EAR TRAINING

TWO NOTE
COMPLETE

by
Bruce Arnold

MUSE EEK

Muse Eek Publishing Company
New York, New York

ISBN 978-1-59489-937-9

Printed in the United States

This publication can be purchased from your local bookstore or by contacting:
Muse Eek Publishing Company
P.O. Box 509
New York, NY 10276, USA
Phone: 212-473-7030
Fax: 212-473-4601
http://www.muse-eek.com
sales@muse-eek.com

Table Of Contents

Acknowledgments

The author would like to thank Michal Shapiro for proof reading and help-ful suggestions.   I would also like to thank my students who through their questions helped me to see their needs so that I might address them as best I could.

About the Author

Bruce Arnold is a guitarist, composer, educator, and author. As a musician, he has achieved a sound that sets him apart by applying jazz improvisational techniques to 20th century-12-tone compositional methods. He has recorded three critically acclaimed CDs that document his unique approach to composition and improvisation, and he has also pioneered the use of the guitar as a controller via the computer program SuperCollider. Bruce co-leads the group Spooky Actions which takes music from sources as far afield as Native American songs to classics by composers such as Webern and Messiaen as vehicles for improvisation. Bruce has a distinguished and versatile performance history, having performed with Stanley Clarke, Joe Pass, Joe Lovano, Randy Brecker, Peter Erskine, Stuart Hamm, the Absolute Ensemble under the baton of Kristjan Järvi,and the Boston Symphony Orchestra. He is the author of over 50 books on music education and directs the groundbreaking NYU Summer Guitar Intensive, which annually brings together the best guitarists in the world to create an inspiring educational environment for the serious student of guitar.

For more information about Mr. Arnold check his website at http://www.brucearnold.com This website contains audio examples of Mr. Arnold's compositions and a workshop section with free downloadable music exercises.

Foreword

There is a direct correlation between a student's ability to identify pitches and their musicality. This ear training series presents a method with which I have had great success in improving my students' abilities to identify pitches, and provides a way to take one more step on the journey toward master musicianship. The course of study presented in this book assumes that the reader has intermediate to advanced knowledge of music.

Bruce Arnold

New York, New York

How to use this book

Congratulations on making it to two note ear training. You should feel proud to know that through hard work you have mastered one note ear training. There are six CDs that are available separately for this book. Please see our website for a list of on-line sources for these disks. Each individual is different. Some students get Two Note ear training right away, but the majority take quite a bit of time. An average student will take between one and two years. With this in mind, keep your spirits high and work every day on this method and you will find that eventually you will develop not only an ability to hear two notes simultaneously but will learn how to hear key modulations.

Let's look at the method you will use to work on Two Note ear training. You will first hear a I IV V I progression in the key of "C" as you did with One Note ear training. Sing or think the tonic note of the key, which would be a "C" note (it is recommend in the beginning to sing the C note until you understand the method better). You will then hear two notes played simultaneously. Continue to sing or think the "C" note. Don't concentrate on the 2 notes you hear but concentrate on the tonic pitch "C" that you are singing. Listen to see if you still hear this C pitch as the tonic For instance if you played a low "Ab" and a high "Eb" against the key of C there is a good chance you might hear these two notes in the key of "Ab". "C" would then sound like the 3rd which would tell you that you have modulated to the key of "Ab".

Whether one stays in the original key of "C" or if one's ear modulates depends on the individual, or sometimes on the note combination or the octave the notes are in. After you have found the key you are in by listening to the "C" note you are singing or hearing, listen to the two notes as you would with the One Note ear training to figure out the pitches. If you have problems hearing the modulation I recommend you first work with "A Key Note Recognition" ISBN #1890944777. This book and separately available CD will help you identify modulations, which is a key part in mastering Two Note ear training. Keep in mind that you won't always hear the key modulation the same way each time when working on Two Note ear training. This is because many two note combinations can be heard in more than one key. When I hear an Eb and a Db a minor seventh above, I commonly hear those pitches in Ab, as the 5th and the 4th. But sometimes I will hear these two notes in Eb, as the "one" and the "flat seven." This is the beauty and the curse of a well developed ear. On one hand the ability to hear pitches in different keys on different days makes for exciting possibilities especially when improvising. On the other hand this makes a more difficult job for your ear, and you need to develop a quick response to which key you think the sound is in. Again the book "A Key Note Recognition will help tremendously to refine this skill.

Over time you may find you are able to hold the "tonic" sound of "C" in your mind without singing it. This is common, and is one more step in obtaining good relative pitch ear training skills.

It is important to sight sing daily along with listening to the Two Note CD. I recommend using "A "Fanatic's Guide to Ear Training and Sight Singing" ISBN #1890944750. A combination of listening to the separately available CD and singing pitches is the key to quick progress with this method.

If you follow the steps I've outlined you can greatly change your perception and accuracy when it comes to pitch recognition and the ability to sight sing melodies. As I have mentioned, some people progress very quickly with this method while for some people it can take years. The important thing is to do the method properly and with dedication, and over time your pitch recognition and sight singing ability will match anyone else's.

Ways to use the Two Note Ear Training CD

The Ear Training CD works best if you use a CD player with shuffle play; this will guarantee that you don't memorize the order of the tracks. Many CD players especially those found in computers will also allow you to choose which tracks you would like to hear. This is particularly helpful if you have problems with certain pitches or certain octaves. The order of Two Note examples are found on the next page. This is useful if you want to make special sequences to work on particular Two Note combinations.

WHAT NEXT?

There are six CDs currently available in the Beginning Level of two note ear training. There are obviously more interval combinations you could work on and I suggest you make your own CDs for this purpose. You can also make 3 note CDs because the process I have shown for 2 notes works for any number of notes.

Names of the Notes found on the Ear Training CD 1

1. D# A#	34. D# A#	67. F C
2. B F#	35. A# F	68. F# C#
3. A# F	36. F# C#	69. G# D#
4. E B	37. C# G#	70. C# G#
5. A E	38. G# D#	71. B F#
6. G# D#	39. B F#	72. D# A#
7. F# C#	40. D A	73. F C
8. C G	41. E B	74. F# C#
9. G D	42. A E	75. G# D#
10. D A	43. F C	76. C# G#
11. A# F	44. D# A#	77. C G
12. A E	45. A# F	78. D A
13. E B	46. G D	79. G D
14. D# A#	47. C G	80. E B
15. F C	48. D A	81. A E
16. B F#	49. B F#	82. A# F
17. C G	50. E B	83. D# A#
18. G D	51. A E	84. B F#
19. A E	52. G# D#	85. F C
20. G# D#	53. C# G#	86. D A
21. F# C#	54. F# C#	87. C G
22. C# G#	55. B F#	88. G D
23. A# F	56. E B	89. F# C#
24. E B	57. A E	90. G# D#
25. A E	58. F C	91. C# G#
26. F C	59. E B	92. E B
27. D# A#	60. A E	93. A E
28. B F#	61. A# F	94. A# F
29. B F#	62. D A	95. G D
30. G D	63. G D	96. C G
31. D A	64. C G	97. D A
32. C G	65. D# A#	98. G# D#
33. F C	66. B F#	99. F# C#

Names of the Notes found on the Ear Training CD 2

1.	E	G#	34.	E	G#	67.	E	G#
2.	A	C#	35.	A	C#	68.	A	C#
3.	A#	D	36.	A#	D	69.	F	A
4.	D	F#	37.	G	B	70.	D#	G
5.	G	B	38.	C	E	71.	B	D#
6.	C	E	39.	D	F#	72.	B	D#
7.	D#	G	40.	G#	C	73.	G	B
8.	B	D#	41.	F#	A#	74.	D	F#
9.	F	A	42.	C#	F	75.	D	F#
10.	F#	A#	43.	F	A	76.	C	E
11.	G#	C	44.	D#	G	77.	F	A
12.	C#	F	45.	B	D#	78.	D#	G
13.	B	D#	46.	A#	D	79.	A#	D
14.	D#	G	47.	E	G#	80.	F#	A#
15.	F	A	48.	A	C#	81.	C#	F
16.	F#	A#	49.	G#	C	82.	G#	C
17.	G#	C	50.	F#	A#	83.	B	D#
18.	C#	F	51.	C	E	84.	E	G#
19.	C	E	52.	G	B	85.	A	C#
20.	D	F#	53.	D	F#	86.	F	A
21.	G	B	54.	A#	D	87.	D#	G
22.	E	G#	55.	A	C#	88.	A#	D
23.	A	C#	56.	E	G#	89.	G	B
24.	A#	D	57.	D#	G	90.	C	E
25.	D#	G	58.	F	A	91.	D	F#
26.	B	D#	59.	B	D#	92.	B	D#
27.	F	A	60.	C	E	93.	E	G#
28.	D	F#	61.	G	B	94.	A	C#
29.	C	E	62.	A	C#	95.	G#	C
30.	G	B	63.	G#	C	96.	C#	F
31.	F#	A#	64.	F#	A#	97.	F#	A#
32.	G#	C	65.	C#	F	98.	B	D#
33.	C#	F	66.	A#	D	99.	E	G#

Names of the Notes found on the Ear Training CD 3

1.	E	C#	34.	D	B	67.	D#	C
2.	A	F	35.	A#	G	68.	A#	G
3.	C	A	36.	A	F#	69.	G	E
4.	B	D#	37.	E	C#	70.	C	A
5.	F	D	38.	D#	C	71.	D	B
6.	F#	D#	39.	F	D	72.	B	G#
7.	G#	F	40.	B	G#	73.	E	C#
8.	C#	A#	41.	C	A	74.	A	F#
9.	B	G#	42.	G	E	75.	G#	F
10.	D#	C	43.	A	F#	76.	C#	A#
11.	F	D	44.	G#	F	77.	F#	D#
12.	F#	D#	45.	F#	D#	78.	B	G#
13.	C#	A#	46.	C#	A#	79.	E	C#
14.	D#	G	47.	A#	G	80.	A	F#
15.	C	A	48.	E	C#	81.	F	D
16.	A	F#	49.	A	F#	82.	D	B
17.	A#	G	50.	F	D	83.	G	E
18.	D#	C	51.	D#	C	84.	C	A
19.	B	G#	52.	G	E	85.	D#	C
20.	F	D	53.	B	G#	86.	B	G#
21.	D	B	54.	B	G#	87.	F	D
22.	C	A	55.	G	E	88.	F#	D#
23.	E	C#	56.	D	B	89.	G#	F
24.	A	F#	57.	F	D	90.	C#	A#
25.	A#	G	58.	D#	C	91.	B	G#
26.	C	A	59.	A#	G	92.	D#	C
27.	F#	D#	60.	F#	D#	93.	F	D
28.	C#	A#	61.	C#	A#	94.	F#	D#
29.	D#	C	62.	G#	F	95.	C#	A#
30.	B	G#	63.	B	G#	96.	C	A
31.	G#	F	64.	E	C#	97.	D	B
32.	F#	D#	65.	A	F#	98.	G#	F
33.	G	E	66.	F	D	99.	E	C#

Names of the Notes found on the Ear Training CD 4

1. E A	34. F# B	67. C F
2. D G	35. C# F#	68. F A#
3. G C	36. F A#	69. D# G#
4. C F	37. D# G#	70. A# D#
5. D# G#	38. A# D#	71. F# B
6. F A#	39. E A	72. C# F#
7. G# C#	40. A D	73. G# C#
8. B E	41. G# C#	74. B E
9. D# G#	42. F# B	75. E A
10. F A#	43. C F	
11. F# B	44. G C	76. A D
12. G# C#	45. D G	77. F A#
13. C F	46. A# D#	78. D# G#
14. D G	47. A D	79. A# D#
15. G C	48. E A	80. G C
16. E A	49. D# G#	81. C F
17. A D	50. F A#	82. D G
18. D# G#	51. B E	83. B E
19. B E	52. C F	84. E A
20. F A#	53. G C	85. A D
21. D G	54. A D	86. G# C#
22. C F	55. G# C#	87. C# F#
23. G C	56. C# F#	88. F# B
24. F# B	57. A# D#	89. B E
25. G# C#	58. E A	90. E A
26. C# F#	59. A D	91. A D
27. E A	60. F A#	92. D# G#
28. A D	61. D# G#	93. G# C#
29. A# D#	62. B E	94. A# D#
30. G C	63. B E	95. D# G#
31. C F	64. G C	96. G# C#
32. D G	65. D G	97. C# F#
33. G# C#	66. D G	98. G C

Names of the Notes found on the Ear Training CD 5

1. E	F#		34. E	F#		67. E	F#
2. A	B		35. A	B		68. A	B
3. A#	C		36. A#	C		69. F	G
4. D	E		37. G	A		70. D#	F
5. G	A		38. C	D		71. B	C#
6. C	D		39. D	E		72. B	C#
7. D#	F		40. G#	A#		73. G	A
8. B	C#		41. F#	G#		74. D	E
9. F	G		42. C#	D#		75. D	E
10. F#	G#		43. F	G		76. C	D
11. G#	A#		44. D#	F		77. F	G
12. G#	C#		45. B	C#		78. D#	F
13. C#	D#		46. A#	C		79. A#	C
14. D#	F		47. E	F#		80. F#	G#
15. F	G		48. A	B		81. C#	D#
16. F#	G#		49. G#	A#		82. G#	A#
17. G#	A#		50. F#	G#		83. B	C#
18. C#	D#		51. C	D		84. E	F#
19. C	D		52. G	A		85. A	B
20. D	E		53. D	E		86. F	G
21. G	A		54. A#	C		87. D#	F
22. E	F#		55. A	B		88. A#	C
23. A	B		56. E	F#		89. G	A
24. A#	C		57. D#	F		90. C	D
25. D#	F		58. F	G		91. D	E
26. B	C#		59. B	C#		92. B	C#
27. F	G		60. C	D		93. E	F#
28. D	E		61. G	A		94. A	B
29. C	D		62. A	B		95. G#	A#
30. G	A		63. G#	A#		96. C#	D#
31. F#	G#		64. F#	G#		97. F#	G#
32. G#	A#		65. C#	D#		98. B	C#
33. C#	D#		66. A#	C		99. E	F#

Names of the Notes found on the Ear Training CD 6

1.	E	D#	34.	E	D#	67.	E	D#
2.	A	G#	35.	A	G#	68.	A	G#
3.	A#	A	36.	A#	A	69.	F	E
4.	D	C#	37.	G	F#	70.	D#	D
5.	G	F#	38.	C	B	71.	B	A#
6.	C	B	39.	D	C#	72.	B	A#
7.	D#	D	40.	G#	G	73.	G	F#
8.	B	A#	41.	F#	F	74.	D	C#
9.	F	E	42.	C#	C	75.	D	C#
10.	F#	F	43.	F	E	76.	C	B
11.	G#	G	44.	D#	D	77.	F	E
12.	C#	C	45.	B	A#	78.	D#	D
13.	B	A#	46.	A#	A	79.	A#	A
14.	D#	D	47.	E	D#	80.	F#	F
15.	F	E	48.	A	G#	81.	C#	C
16.	F#	F	49.	G#	G	82.	G#	G
17.	G#	G	50.	F#	F	83.	B	A#
18.	C#	C	51.	C	B	84.	E	D#
19.	C	B	52.	G	F#	85.	A	G#
20.	D	C#	53.	D	C#	86.	F	E
21.	G	F#	54.	A#	A	87.	D#	D
22.	E	D#	55.	A	G#	88.	A#	A
23.	A	G#	56.	E	D#	89.	G	F#
24.	A#	A	57.	D#	D	90.	C	B
25.	D#	D	58.	F	E	91.	D	C#
26.	B	A#	59.	B	A#	92.	B	A#
27.	F	E	60.	C	B	93.	E	D#
28.	D	C#	61.	G	F#	94.	A	G#
29.	C	B	62.	A	G#	95.	G#	G
30.	G	F#	63.	G#	G	96.	C#	C
31.	F#	F	64.	F#	F	97.	F#	F
32.	G#	G	65.	C#	C	98.	B	A#
33.	C#	C	66.	A#	A	99.	E	D#

Frequently Asked Questions

It is strongly recommended that you read through these questions that various students have submitted. Although this method of ear training is simple in concept, it is easy to do it incorrectly either through previous misleading musical training or just a misunderstanding on your part. If you don't proceed with this ear training with a good grasp of the concept, you will find that sooner or later you will hit a wall. The questions found here relate specifically to the following books: "Fanatic's Guide to Sight Singing and Ear Training," and "Ear Training Two Note Complete" book series.

I've been working on "Ear Training: Two Note Volume One Beginning" and I'm having a hard time hearing how the key center changes. Could you suggest anything to help?

There are quite a few approaches you can use to help yourself when you have problems changing keys. For one thing two notes don't define a key as well as three or four in some instances. Therefore two note ear training can be harder than three or four note ear training. You should keep in mind that once this "hearing the key" hurdle is over, you will find that three, four or more note combinations will usually be quite easy. This of course depends on the note combination but any note combination that closely outlines a typical chord sound will set up a key center so strongly that you will hear the key almost immediately. It is not uncommon for a student to take a year or two before they feel they have a handle on hearing the key change with the C note they are singing. Here is the incentive: once this happens you progress at a much quicker pace.

There are several things that can keep a student from developing this key change ability. I've made a list below of how to address some of the common problems associated with not hearing the key center change.

1. Many students will raise or lower the C they are singing without even realizing it. Make sure to take a deep breath before each exercise to help support singing the C.

2. Concentrate more on the note you are singing than on the 2 notes that are being played. Have faith that you will modulate to a new key if the 2 notes dictate this. You should spend your concentration on the sound of the C and whether it has changed keys. Remember that the most important thing is to know what key you are in. Without this information you are totally lost.

3. Always review the "Key Note Recognition" CD to make sure you are maintaining 100% accuracy.

4. Remember that you won't hear every example the same way every day. Some days a particular example may modulate and on other days in might not. Also if you are doing this ear training with a friend don't expect that you will hear the same key as they do. Depending upon your musical background and the type of music you listen to it is not uncommon for a classical musician for instance, to hear a tritone differently than a blues musician.

You recommend singing the tonic of the key. I don't understand how I can use this when I'm on stage to hear modulations. Please explain.

As your key retention builds you will find that you don't have to sing the C note; you will just think it. After even more time your sense of key will be so natural that you will have an automatic response to a key change. This can take years to develop, but it does happen.

I've been noticing that when I hear the two notes sound I hear the C as the 5th. When I listen to the two note CD with the 3rds I hear the C as the 3rd a lot. Of course I have the wrong answer but maybe you could help me out?

It is very common for students to confuse the note they are singing with the interval sound of the two notes. This is a place where previous interval training can really mess you up. I find that students with a lot of previous interval training have a much harder time with two note ear training. Basically you have to unlearn hearing intervals and start hearing the key degree of the note you are singing. I find that a lot of singing exercises like the ones found in the "Fanatic's Guide" can help this problem but diligent practice and concentration are also extremely important in breaking bad habits like this.

How well should I have each of the two note CDs down before moving on to the next?

Unlike the one note ear training and the key note recognition ear training, two note ear training doesn't have to be 100% accurate before moving on to the next CD; 80% accuracy is sufficient. You will find as you progress that many two or more note combinations that you have had problems with will become clear.

I've been working with your ear training for 3 years now and feel very good about my progress. I can sing all the exercises in the "Fanatic's Guide" and was wondering if you could recommend some other singing exercises?

I would recommend three of my books for further singing exercises. "LINES" and Volumes One and Two of "Single String Studies for Guitar." "LINES" is a book for part singing. You will have 4 voices happening at the same time and you need to sing one of the voices. You will find this very challenging especially to maintain your internal sense of the key center. I recommend "Single String Studies for Guitar Volumes One and Two" even if you aren't a guitar player. These two books present you with a page of random notes that you should sing. Volume one presents a page of random notes in every key. You should first attempt to sing the page of notes in whatever key is listed and use the "Fanatic's Guide" CD as a drone. You will also have to change octaves on many notes but this is good practice anyway. After you feel comfortable singing with the "Fanatic's Guide" CD you should give yourself a key center by either playing the "Fanatic's Guide" CD or a chording instrument. But this time you should try to sing the entire page in the key without hearing the drone. It can be very challenging, but to hold onto the key while singing the notes is a great exercise and will go a long way toward helping you improve your key retention. After you have completed the book using this method you should also try to sing a page that is in the key of C but try to sing it in the key of F#. It is very challenging to keep the C key center while singing notes that are diatonic to F#. Singing each page in every key will keep you busy for quite some time. Volume Two of "Single String Studies" presents you with 12 tone lines which should be practiced in the same way and order as you did with Volume One. Overall you will find these two books to be a real sight singing challenge.

I may be getting ahead of myself but could you tell me how I will be able to hear 4 voices moving at once. For instances if you had a four note chord moving to another 4 note chord?

This can be easier than you might think. Once you can hear two or three notes and identify the key and the notes you hear, you will find that when hearing a chord progression containing 4 notes per voicing, you are able to concentrate on the outer and inner voices and hear how they are sounding within the key. If you want to use a controlled method to develop this skill I recommend you work out of the book "LINES."

I'm getting about 80% right on the two note CD but I have a few examples where I just don't hear the C as anything. Could you recommend anything to help?

Students frequently find there are a few combinations of notes for which they can't hear the key change or can't separate the notes found in the two note combination. If you are getting 80% right answers I would suggest you move on to other volumes of the two note ear training or make your own three note tapes/CDs. In most cases if you come back to those examples after working further into the method you will find that you can now understand and hear them.

I have problems separating the two notes. It's weird but they almost sound like one fused sound which I can't seem to separate out into separate pitches. Can you explain this or offer any advice?

It is common for students to have this problem. One of the reasons for this is that you haven't developed your sense of the uniqueness of each sound within a key to a point that it can separate out individual sounds within a key that are sounding simultaneously. You will find that over time this will go away; but it can be quite frustrating at the beginning. This is one of the main reasons why the two note books start with certain interval combinations. Most students find it easier to hear two distinct pitches with 5ths or 3rds than they do with 2nds. Eventually you will find these fused notes will separate as you begin to distinguish their characteristic sound within a key. Commonly people that have done interval training will also have this problem because they just hear an interval but are unable to separate the sounds into what their function is within the key center. If you have done a lot of interval training be patient with yourself because it will take an extra long time for this problem to work itself out.

How do you recommend I practice the two note ear training method?

I would use the same principle as you used with one note ear training and key note recognition. Practice many times throughout the day in short 10 to 15 minute practice sessions. I also find as you enter into two or more note ear training it becomes increasingly important to be working on singing exercises at the same time. Working through the "Fanatic's Guide," "Lines" and the "Single String Studies" books is important to help your ear develop the ability to hear key centers in a variety of different musical settings.

I realize your books are very good for developing your ear training skills but can you recommend some exercises that I can do with the music I play. Maybe like jazz standards or something like that?

Once my students have worked with the "Fanatic's Guide" to a point where they can pretty much sing anything in the book correctly, I also give them exercises singing jazz standards. This is done in a number of ways. You can try any of these:

1. Take a tune that pretty much sticks to one key like "Bye Bye Blackbird" or "It Could Happen to You" and sing the melody while playing the bass note of each chord. (Make sure to first give yourself a cadence in the key of the tune).

2. Play the melody of a standard and sing the bass notes.

3. Sing 7th chords for each chord of the tune and try to maintain the key. Once again start with songs that don't modulate.

Try singing all these combinations:

1,3,5,7	3,1,5,7	5,1,3,7	7,1,3,5
1,3,7,5	3,1,7,5	5,1,7,3	7,1,4,1
1,5,3,7	3,5,1,7	5,3,1,7	7,3,1,5
1,5,7,3	3,5,7,1	5,3,7,1	7,3,5,1
1,7,3,5	3,7,1,5	5,7,1,3	7,5,1,3
1,7,5,3	3,7,5,1	5,7,3,1	7,5,3,1

As you feel more comfortable with tunes that stay in one key, branch out to songs that modulate. Try singing more complicated melodies like be-bop tunes and transcribed solos. I would also highly recommend working with classical pieces. Start with Baroque music and work your way to 20th century classical music. Remember everything is in a key but it may take quite some time to really hear it.

Could you give me a rough idea of how long it should take me to complete your ear training method.

My first response is: your entire life. Through this ear training method I have given you the path to having a great ear. You need to stay on that path and challenge your ears every day to improve. Whether you are using one of my books or listening to and playing music you need to continue to build your ability. You can always be faster at whatever skill you obtain with this method. You will always find some unusual combination of sounds that throws you a curve. I find the musicians that really excel with this method make ear training a permanent part of their practice regimen. Those that get kind of good at two note ear training and then stop are usually back to where they started in a few years. It's as if you learned a foreign language and then never spoke it; you are going to forget large chunks because you aren't using it. The sooner you can start applying this ear training to your everyday interaction with sound the better off you will be.

You can use this log to keep track of which two note combination are causing you problems. I would spend extra time on any combination of notes that you consistently get wrong.

Note Combination _____   Answer given_____   Correct Answer_____
Note Combination _____   Answer given_____   Correct Answer_____
Note Combination _____   Answer given_____   Correct Answer_____
Note Combination _____   Answer given_____   Correct Answer_____
Note Combination _____   Answer given_____   Correct Answer_____
Note Combination _____   Answer given_____   Correct Answer_____
Note Combination _____   Answer given_____   Correct Answer_____
Note Combination _____   Answer given_____   Correct Answer_____
Note Combination _____   Answer given_____   Correct Answer_____
Note Combination _____   Answer given_____   Correct Answer_____
Note Combination _____   Answer given_____   Correct Answer_____
Note Combination _____   Answer given_____   Correct Answer_____
Note Combination _____   Answer given_____   Correct Answer_____
Note Combination _____   Answer given_____   Correct Answer_____
Note Combination _____   Answer given_____   Correct Answer_____
Note Combination _____   Answer given_____   Correct Answer_____
Note Combination _____   Answer given_____   Correct Answer_____
Note Combination _____   Answer given_____   Correct Answer_____
Note Combination _____   Answer given_____   Correct Answer_____
Note Combination _____   Answer given_____   Correct Answer_____
Note Combination _____   Answer given_____   Correct Answer_____
Note Combination _____   Answer given_____   Correct Answer_____
Note Combination _____   Answer given_____   Correct Answer_____
Note Combination _____   Answer given_____   Correct Answer_____
Note Combination _____   Answer given_____   Correct Answer_____
Note Combination _____   Answer given_____   Correct Answer_____
Note Combination _____   Answer given_____   Correct Answer_____
Note Combination _____   Answer given_____   Correct Answer_____
Note Combination _____   Answer given_____   Correct Answer_____
Note Combination _____   Answer given_____   Correct Answer_____
Note Combination _____   Answer given_____   Correct Answer_____
Note Combination _____   Answer given_____   Correct Answer_____
Note Combination _____   Answer given_____   Correct Answer_____
Note Combination _____   Answer given_____   Correct Answer_____
Note Combination _____   Answer given_____   Correct Answer_____
Note Combination _____   Answer given_____   Correct Answer_____
Note Combination _____   Answer given_____   Correct Answer_____
Note Combination _____   Answer given_____   Correct Answer_____
Note Combination _____   Answer given_____   Correct Answer_____

Note Combination _____ Answer given_____ Correct Answer_____

Note Combination _____ Answer given_____ Correct Answer_____

Note Combination _____ Answer given_____ Correct Answer_____

Note Combination _____ Answer given_____ Correct Answer_____

Note Combination _____ Answer given_____ Correct Answer_____

Note Combination _____ Answer given_____ Correct Answer_____

Note Combination _____ Answer given_____ Correct Answer_____

Note Combination _____ Answer given_____ Correct Answer_____

Note Combination _____ Answer given_____ Correct Answer_____

Note Combination _____ Answer given_____ Correct Answer_____

Note Combination _____ Answer given_____ Correct Answer_____

Note Combination _____ Answer given_____ Correct Answer_____

Note Combination _____ Answer given_____ Correct Answer_____

Note Combination _____ Answer given_____ Correct Answer_____

Note Combination _____ Answer given_____ Correct Answer_____

Note Combination _____ Answer given_____ Correct Answer_____

Note Combination _____ Answer given_____ Correct Answer_____

Note Combination _____ Answer given_____ Correct Answer_____

Note Combination _____ Answer given_____ Correct Answer_____

Note Combination _____ Answer given_____ Correct Answer_____

Note Combination _____ Answer given_____ Correct Answer_____

Note Combination _____ Answer given_____ Correct Answer_____

Note Combination _____ Answer given_____ Correct Answer_____

Note Combination _____ Answer given_____ Correct Answer_____

Note Combination _____ Answer given_____ Correct Answer_____

Note Combination _____ Answer given_____ Correct Answer_____

Note Combination _____ Answer given_____ Correct Answer_____

Note Combination _____ Answer given_____ Correct Answer_____

Note Combination _____ Answer given_____ Correct Answer_____

Note Combination _____ Answer given_____ Correct Answer_____

Note Combination _____ Answer given_____ Correct Answer_____

Note Combination _____ Answer given_____ Correct Answer_____

Note Combination _____ Answer given_____ Correct Answer_____

Note Combination _____ Answer given_____ Correct Answer_____

Note Combination _____ Answer given_____ Correct Answer_____

Note Combination _____ Answer given_____ Correct Answer_____

Note Combination _____ Answer given_____ Correct Answer_____

Note Combination _____ Answer given_____ Correct Answer_____

Note Combination _____ Answer given_____ Correct Answer_____

Note Combination _____ Answer given_____ Correct Answer_____

Note Combination _____ Answer given_____ Correct Answer_____

Note Combination _____ Answer given_____ Correct Answer_____

Note Combination _____ Answer given_____ Correct Answer_____

Note Combination _____ Answer given_____ Correct Answer_____

Note Combination _____ Answer given_____ Correct Answer_____

Note Combination _____ Answer given_____ Correct Answer_____

Note Combination _____ Answer given_____ Correct Answer_____

Note Combination _____ Answer given_____ Correct Answer_____

Note Combination _____ Answer given_____ Correct Answer_____

Note Combination _____ Answer given_____ Correct Answer_____

Note Combination _____ Answer given_____ Correct Answer_____

Note Combination _____ Answer given_____ Correct Answer_____

Note Combination _____ Answer given_____ Correct Answer_____

Note Combination _____ Answer given_____ Correct Answer_____

Note Combination _____ Answer given_____ Correct Answer_____

Note Combination _____ Answer given_____ Correct Answer_____

Note Combination _____ Answer given_____ Correct Answer_____

Note Combination _____ Answer given_____ Correct Answer_____

Note Combination _____ Answer given_____ Correct Answer_____

Note Combination _____ Answer given_____ Correct Answer_____

Note Combination _____ Answer given_____ Correct Answer_____

Note Combination _____ Answer given_____ Correct Answer_____

Note Combination _____ Answer given_____ Correct Answer_____

Note Combination _____ Answer given_____ Correct Answer_____

Note Combination _____ Answer given_____ Correct Answer_____

Note Combination _____ Answer given_____ Correct Answer_____

Note Combination _____ Answer given_____ Correct Answer_____

Note Combination _____ Answer given_____ Correct Answer_____

Note Combination _____ Answer given_____ Correct Answer_____

Note Combination _____ Answer given_____ Correct Answer_____

Note Combination _____ Answer given_____ Correct Answer_____

Note Combination _____ Answer given_____ Correct Answer_____

Note Combination _____ Answer given_____ Correct Answer_____

Note Combination _____ Answer given_____ Correct Answer_____

Note Combination _____ Answer given_____ Correct Answer_____

Note Combination _____ Answer given_____ Correct Answer_____

Note Combination _____ Answer given_____ Correct Answer_____

Note Combination _____ Answer given_____ Correct Answer_____

Note Combination _____ Answer given_____ Correct Answer_____

Note Combination _____ Answer given_____ Correct Answer_____

Note Combination _____ Answer given_____ Correct Answer_____

Note Combination _____   Answer given_____   Correct Answer_____

Note Combination _____   Answer given_____   Correct Answer_____

Note Combination _____   Answer given_____   Correct Answer_____

Note Combination _____   Answer given_____   Correct Answer_____

Note Combination _____   Answer given_____   Correct Answer_____

Note Combination _____   Answer given_____   Correct Answer_____

Note Combination _____   Answer given_____   Correct Answer_____

Note Combination _____   Answer given_____   Correct Answer_____

Note Combination _____   Answer given_____   Correct Answer_____

Note Combination _____   Answer given_____   Correct Answer_____

Note Combination _____   Answer given_____   Correct Answer_____

Note Combination _____   Answer given_____   Correct Answer_____

Note Combination _____   Answer given_____   Correct Answer_____

Note Combination _____   Answer given_____   Correct Answer_____

Note Combination _____   Answer given_____   Correct Answer_____

Note Combination _____   Answer given_____   Correct Answer_____

Note Combination _____   Answer given_____   Correct Answer_____

Note Combination _____   Answer given_____   Correct Answer_____

Note Combination _____   Answer given_____   Correct Answer_____

Note Combination _____   Answer given_____   Correct Answer_____

Note Combination _____   Answer given_____   Correct Answer_____

Note Combination _____   Answer given_____   Correct Answer_____

Note Combination _____   Answer given_____   Correct Answer_____

Note Combination _____   Answer given_____   Correct Answer_____

Note Combination _____   Answer given_____   Correct Answer_____

Note Combination _____   Answer given_____   Correct Answer_____

Note Combination _____   Answer given_____   Correct Answer_____

Note Combination _____   Answer given_____   Correct Answer_____

Note Combination _____   Answer given_____   Correct Answer_____

Note Combination _____   Answer given_____   Correct Answer_____

Note Combination _____   Answer given_____   Correct Answer_____

Note Combination _____   Answer given_____   Correct Answer_____

Note Combination _____   Answer given_____   Correct Answer_____

Note Combination _____   Answer given_____   Correct Answer_____

Note Combination _____   Answer given_____   Correct Answer_____

Note Combination _____   Answer given_____   Correct Answer_____

Note Combination _____   Answer given_____   Correct Answer_____

Note Combination _____   Answer given_____   Correct Answer_____

Note Combination _____   Answer given_____   Correct Answer_____

Note Combination _____   Answer given_____   Correct Answer_____

Note Combination _____	Answer given_____	Correct Answer_____
Note Combination _____	Answer given_____	Correct Answer_____
Note Combination _____	Answer given_____	Correct Answer_____
Note Combination _____	Answer given_____	Correct Answer_____
Note Combination _____	Answer given_____	Correct Answer_____
Note Combination _____	Answer given_____	Correct Answer_____
Note Combination _____	Answer given_____	Correct Answer_____
Note Combination _____	Answer given_____	Correct Answer_____
Note Combination _____	Answer given_____	Correct Answer_____
Note Combination _____	Answer given_____	Correct Answer_____
Note Combination _____	Answer given_____	Correct Answer_____
Note Combination _____	Answer given_____	Correct Answer_____
Note Combination _____	Answer given_____	Correct Answer_____
Note Combination _____	Answer given_____	Correct Answer_____
Note Combination _____	Answer given_____	Correct Answer_____
Note Combination _____	Answer given_____	Correct Answer_____
Note Combination _____	Answer given_____	Correct Answer_____
Note Combination _____	Answer given_____	Correct Answer_____
Note Combination _____	Answer given_____	Correct Answer_____
Note Combination _____	Answer given_____	Correct Answer_____
Note Combination _____	Answer given_____	Correct Answer_____
Note Combination _____	Answer given_____	Correct Answer_____
Note Combination _____	Answer given_____	Correct Answer_____
Note Combination _____	Answer given_____	Correct Answer_____
Note Combination _____	Answer given_____	Correct Answer_____
Note Combination _____	Answer given_____	Correct Answer_____
Note Combination _____	Answer given_____	Correct Answer_____
Note Combination _____	Answer given_____	Correct Answer_____
Note Combination _____	Answer given_____	Correct Answer_____
Note Combination _____	Answer given_____	Correct Answer_____
Note Combination _____	Answer given_____	Correct Answer_____
Note Combination _____	Answer given_____	Correct Answer_____
Note Combination _____	Answer given_____	Correct Answer_____
Note Combination _____	Answer given_____	Correct Answer_____
Note Combination _____	Answer given_____	Correct Answer_____
Note Combination _____	Answer given_____	Correct Answer_____
Note Combination _____	Answer given_____	Correct Answer_____
Note Combination _____	Answer given_____	Correct Answer_____
Note Combination _____	Answer given_____	Correct Answer_____

Note Combination _____   Answer given_____   Correct Answer_____
Note Combination _____   Answer given_____   Correct Answer_____
Note Combination _____   Answer given_____   Correct Answer_____
Note Combination _____   Answer given_____   Correct Answer_____
Note Combination _____   Answer given_____   Correct Answer_____
Note Combination _____   Answer given_____   Correct Answer_____
Note Combination _____   Answer given_____   Correct Answer_____
Note Combination _____   Answer given_____   Correct Answer_____
Note Combination _____   Answer given_____   Correct Answer_____
Note Combination _____   Answer given_____   Correct Answer_____
Note Combination _____   Answer given_____   Correct Answer_____
Note Combination _____   Answer given_____   Correct Answer_____
Note Combination _____   Answer given_____   Correct Answer_____
Note Combination _____   Answer given_____   Correct Answer_____
Note Combination _____   Answer given_____   Correct Answer_____
Note Combination _____   Answer given_____   Correct Answer_____
Note Combination _____   Answer given_____   Correct Answer_____
Note Combination _____   Answer given_____   Correct Answer_____
Note Combination _____   Answer given_____   Correct Answer_____
Note Combination _____   Answer given_____   Correct Answer_____
Note Combination _____   Answer given_____   Correct Answer_____
Note Combination _____   Answer given_____   Correct Answer_____
Note Combination _____   Answer given_____   Correct Answer_____
Note Combination _____   Answer given_____   Correct Answer_____
Note Combination _____   Answer given_____   Correct Answer_____
Note Combination _____   Answer given_____   Correct Answer_____
Note Combination _____   Answer given_____   Correct Answer_____
Note Combination _____   Answer given_____   Correct Answer_____
Note Combination _____   Answer given_____   Correct Answer_____
Note Combination _____   Answer given_____   Correct Answer_____
Note Combination _____   Answer given_____   Correct Answer_____
Note Combination _____   Answer given_____   Correct Answer_____
Note Combination _____   Answer given_____   Correct Answer_____
Note Combination _____   Answer given_____   Correct Answer_____
Note Combination _____   Answer given_____   Correct Answer_____
Note Combination _____   Answer given_____   Correct Answer_____
Note Combination _____   Answer given_____   Correct Answer_____
Note Combination _____   Answer given_____   Correct Answer_____

Note Combination _____ Answer given_____ Correct Answer_____

Note Combination _____ Answer given_____ Correct Answer_____

Note Combination _____ Answer given_____ Correct Answer_____

Note Combination _____ Answer given_____ Correct Answer_____

Note Combination _____ Answer given_____ Correct Answer_____

Note Combination _____ Answer given_____ Correct Answer_____

Note Combination _____ Answer given_____ Correct Answer_____

Note Combination _____ Answer given_____ Correct Answer_____

Note Combination _____ Answer given_____ Correct Answer_____

Note Combination _____ Answer given_____ Correct Answer_____

Note Combination _____ Answer given_____ Correct Answer_____

Note Combination _____ Answer given_____ Correct Answer_____

Note Combination _____ Answer given_____ Correct Answer_____

Note Combination _____ Answer given_____ Correct Answer_____

Note Combination _____ Answer given_____ Correct Answer_____

Note Combination _____ Answer given_____ Correct Answer_____

Note Combination _____ Answer given_____ Correct Answer_____

Note Combination _____ Answer given_____ Correct Answer_____

Note Combination _____ Answer given_____ Correct Answer_____

Note Combination _____ Answer given_____ Correct Answer_____

Note Combination _____ Answer given_____ Correct Answer_____

Note Combination _____ Answer given_____ Correct Answer_____

Note Combination _____ Answer given_____ Correct Answer_____

Note Combination _____ Answer given_____ Correct Answer_____

Note Combination _____ Answer given_____ Correct Answer_____

Note Combination _____ Answer given_____ Correct Answer_____

Note Combination _____ Answer given_____ Correct Answer_____

Note Combination _____ Answer given_____ Correct Answer_____

Note Combination _____ Answer given_____ Correct Answer_____

Note Combination _____ Answer given_____ Correct Answer_____

Note Combination _____ Answer given_____ Correct Answer_____

Note Combination _____ Answer given_____ Correct Answer_____

Note Combination _____ Answer given_____ Correct Answer_____

Note Combination _____ Answer given_____ Correct Answer_____

Note Combination _____ Answer given_____ Correct Answer_____

Note Combination _____ Answer given_____ Correct Answer_____

Note Combination _____ Answer given_____ Correct Answer_____

Note Combination _____ Answer given_____ Correct Answer_____

Note Combination _____ Answer given_____ Correct Answer_____

Note Combination _____ Answer given_____ Correct Answer_____

Note Combination _____   Answer given_____   Correct Answer_____
Note Combination _____   Answer given_____   Correct Answer_____
Note Combination _____   Answer given_____   Correct Answer_____
Note Combination _____   Answer given_____   Correct Answer_____
Note Combination _____   Answer given_____   Correct Answer_____
Note Combination _____   Answer given_____   Correct Answer_____
Note Combination _____   Answer given_____   Correct Answer_____
Note Combination _____   Answer given_____   Correct Answer_____
Note Combination _____   Answer given_____   Correct Answer_____
Note Combination _____   Answer given_____   Correct Answer_____
Note Combination _____   Answer given_____   Correct Answer_____
Note Combination _____   Answer given_____   Correct Answer_____
Note Combination _____   Answer given_____   Correct Answer_____
Note Combination _____   Answer given_____   Correct Answer_____
Note Combination _____   Answer given_____   Correct Answer_____
Note Combination _____   Answer given_____   Correct Answer_____
Note Combination _____   Answer given_____   Correct Answer_____
Note Combination _____   Answer given_____   Correct Answer_____
Note Combination _____   Answer given_____   Correct Answer_____
Note Combination _____   Answer given_____   Correct Answer_____
Note Combination _____   Answer given_____   Correct Answer_____
Note Combination _____   Answer given_____   Correct Answer_____
Note Combination _____   Answer given_____   Correct Answer_____
Note Combination _____   Answer given_____   Correct Answer_____
Note Combination _____   Answer given_____   Correct Answer_____
Note Combination _____   Answer given_____   Correct Answer_____
Note Combination _____   Answer given_____   Correct Answer_____
Note Combination _____   Answer given_____   Correct Answer_____
Note Combination _____   Answer given_____   Correct Answer_____
Note Combination _____   Answer given_____   Correct Answer_____
Note Combination _____   Answer given_____   Correct Answer_____
Note Combination _____   Answer given_____   Correct Answer_____
Note Combination _____   Answer given_____   Correct Answer_____
Note Combination _____   Answer given_____   Correct Answer_____
Note Combination _____   Answer given_____   Correct Answer_____
Note Combination _____   Answer given_____   Correct Answer_____
Note Combination _____   Answer given_____   Correct Answer_____
Note Combination _____   Answer given_____   Correct Answer_____
Note Combination _____   Answer given_____   Correct Answer_____
Note Combination _____   Answer given_____   Correct Answer_____
Note Combination _____   Answer given_____   Correct Answer_____
Note Combination _____   Answer given_____   Correct Answer_____
Note Combination _____   Answer given_____   Correct Answer_____
Note Combination _____   Answer given_____   Correct Answer_____

Note Combination _____	Answer given_____	Correct Answer_____
Note Combination _____	Answer given_____	Correct Answer_____
Note Combination _____	Answer given_____	Correct Answer_____
Note Combination _____	Answer given_____	Correct Answer_____
Note Combination _____	Answer given_____	Correct Answer_____
Note Combination _____	Answer given_____	Correct Answer_____
Note Combination _____	Answer given_____	Correct Answer_____
Note Combination _____	Answer given_____	Correct Answer_____
Note Combination _____	Answer given_____	Correct Answer_____
Note Combination _____	Answer given_____	Correct Answer_____
Note Combination _____	Answer given_____	Correct Answer_____
Note Combination _____	Answer given_____	Correct Answer_____
Note Combination _____	Answer given_____	Correct Answer_____
Note Combination _____	Answer given_____	Correct Answer_____
Note Combination _____	Answer given_____	Correct Answer_____
Note Combination _____	Answer given_____	Correct Answer_____
Note Combination _____	Answer given_____	Correct Answer_____
Note Combination _____	Answer given_____	Correct Answer_____
Note Combination _____	Answer given_____	Correct Answer_____
Note Combination _____	Answer given_____	Correct Answer_____
Note Combination _____	Answer given_____	Correct Answer_____
Note Combination _____	Answer given_____	Correct Answer_____
Note Combination _____	Answer given_____	Correct Answer_____
Note Combination _____	Answer given_____	Correct Answer_____
Note Combination _____	Answer given_____	Correct Answer_____
Note Combination _____	Answer given_____	Correct Answer_____
Note Combination _____	Answer given_____	Correct Answer_____
Note Combination _____	Answer given_____	Correct Answer_____
Note Combination _____	Answer given_____	Correct Answer_____
Note Combination _____	Answer given_____	Correct Answer_____
Note Combination _____	Answer given_____	Correct Answer_____
Note Combination _____	Answer given_____	Correct Answer_____
Note Combination _____	Answer given_____	Correct Answer_____
Note Combination _____	Answer given_____	Correct Answer_____
Note Combination _____	Answer given_____	Correct Answer_____
Note Combination _____	Answer given_____	Correct Answer_____
Note Combination _____	Answer given_____	Correct Answer_____
Note Combination _____	Answer given_____	Correct Answer_____
Note Combination _____	Answer given_____	Correct Answer_____

Note Combination _____   Answer given_____   Correct Answer_____

Note Combination _____   Answer given_____   Correct Answer_____

Note Combination _____   Answer given_____   Correct Answer_____

Note Combination _____   Answer given_____   Correct Answer_____

Note Combination _____   Answer given_____   Correct Answer_____

Note Combination _____   Answer given_____   Correct Answer_____

Note Combination _____   Answer given_____   Correct Answer_____

Note Combination _____   Answer given_____   Correct Answer_____

Note Combination _____   Answer given_____   Correct Answer_____

Note Combination _____   Answer given_____   Correct Answer_____

Note Combination _____   Answer given_____   Correct Answer_____

Note Combination _____   Answer given_____   Correct Answer_____

Note Combination _____   Answer given_____   Correct Answer_____

Note Combination _____   Answer given_____   Correct Answer_____

Note Combination _____   Answer given_____   Correct Answer_____

Note Combination _____   Answer given_____   Correct Answer_____

Note Combination _____   Answer given_____   Correct Answer_____

Note Combination _____   Answer given_____   Correct Answer_____

Note Combination _____   Answer given_____   Correct Answer_____

Note Combination _____   Answer given_____   Correct Answer_____

Note Combination _____   Answer given_____   Correct Answer_____

Note Combination _____   Answer given_____   Correct Answer_____

Note Combination _____   Answer given_____   Correct Answer_____

Note Combination _____   Answer given_____   Correct Answer_____

Note Combination _____   Answer given_____   Correct Answer_____

Note Combination _____   Answer given_____   Correct Answer_____

Note Combination _____   Answer given_____   Correct Answer_____

Note Combination _____   Answer given_____   Correct Answer_____

Note Combination _____   Answer given_____   Correct Answer_____

Note Combination _____   Answer given_____   Correct Answer_____

Note Combination _____   Answer given_____   Correct Answer_____

Note Combination _____   Answer given_____   Correct Answer_____

Note Combination _____   Answer given_____   Correct Answer_____

Note Combination _____   Answer given_____   Correct Answer_____

Note Combination _____   Answer given_____   Correct Answer_____

Note Combination _____   Answer given_____   Correct Answer_____

Note Combination _____   Answer given_____   Correct Answer_____

Note Combination _____   Answer given_____   Correct Answer_____

Note Combination _____   Answer given_____   Correct Answer_____

Note Combination _____   Answer given_____   Correct Answer_____

Note Combination _____   Answer given_____   Correct Answer_____

Note Combination _____   Answer given_____   Correct Answer_____

Note Combination _____   Answer given_____   Correct Answer_____

Note Combination _____   Answer given_____   Correct Answer_____

Note Combination _____   Answer given_____   Correct Answer_____

Note Combination _____   Answer given_____   Correct Answer_____

Note Combination _____   Answer given_____   Correct Answer_____

Note Combination _____   Answer given_____   Correct Answer_____

Note Combination _____   Answer given_____   Correct Answer_____

Note Combination _____   Answer given_____   Correct Answer_____

Note Combination _____   Answer given_____   Correct Answer_____

Note Combination _____   Answer given_____   Correct Answer_____

Note Combination _____   Answer given_____   Correct Answer_____

Note Combination _____   Answer given_____   Correct Answer_____

Note Combination _____   Answer given_____   Correct Answer_____

Note Combination _____   Answer given_____   Correct Answer_____

Note Combination _____   Answer given_____   Correct Answer_____

Note Combination _____   Answer given_____   Correct Answer_____

Note Combination _____   Answer given_____   Correct Answer_____

Note Combination _____   Answer given_____   Correct Answer_____

Note Combination _____   Answer given_____   Correct Answer_____

Note Combination _____   Answer given_____   Correct Answer_____

Note Combination _____   Answer given_____   Correct Answer_____

Note Combination _____   Answer given_____   Correct Answer_____

Note Combination _____   Answer given_____   Correct Answer_____

Note Combination _____   Answer given_____   Correct Answer_____

Note Combination _____   Answer given_____   Correct Answer_____

Note Combination _____   Answer given_____   Correct Answer_____

Note Combination _____   Answer given_____   Correct Answer_____

Note Combination _____   Answer given_____   Correct Answer_____

Note Combination _____   Answer given_____   Correct Answer_____

Note Combination _____   Answer given_____   Correct Answer_____

Note Combination _____   Answer given_____   Correct Answer_____

Note Combination _____   Answer given_____   Correct Answer_____

Note Combination _____   Answer given_____   Correct Answer_____

Note Combination _____   Answer given_____   Correct Answer_____

Note Combination _____   Answer given_____   Correct Answer_____

Note Combination _____   Answer given_____   Correct Answer_____

Note Combination _____   Answer given_____   Correct Answer_____

Note Combination _____   Answer given_____   Correct Answer_____

Note Combination _____   Answer given_____   Correct Answer_____

The Bruce Arnold series of instruction books for guitar are the result of 30 years of teaching. Mr. Arnold, who teaches at New York University and Princeton University has listened to the questions and problems of his students, and written over fifty books addressing the needs of the beginning to advanced student. Written in a direct, friendly and practical manner, each book is structured in such a way as to enable a student to understand, retain and apply musical information. In short, these books teach.

1st Steps for a Beginning Guitarist
Perfect Bound ISBN 1890944-93-9

1st Steps for a Beginning Guitarist is a comprehensive method for guitar students who have no prior musical training. Whether you are playing acoustic, electric or twelve-string guitar, this book will give you the information you need, and trouble shoot the various pitfalls that can hinder the self-taught musician. Includes pictures, videos and audio in the form of midifiles and mp3's.

Chord Workbook for Guitar Volume 1 (2nd edition)
Perfect Bound ISBN 1890944-50-5

A consistent seller, this book addresses the needs of the beginning through intermediate student. The beginning student will learn chords on the guitar, and a section is also included to help learn the basics of music theory. Progressions are provided to help the student apply these chords to common sequences. The more advanced student will find the reharmonization section to be an invaluable resource of harmonic choices. Information is given through musical notation as well as tablature.

Chord Workbook for Guitar Volume 2 (2nd edition)
Perfect Bound ISBN 1890944-51-3

This book is the Rosetta Stone of pop/jazz chords, and is geared to the intermediate to advanced student. These are the chords that any serious student bent on a musical career must know. Unlike other books which simply give examples of isolated chords, this unique book provides a comprehensive series of progressions and chord combinations which are immediately applicable to both composition and performance.

Music Theory Workbook for Guitar Series

The worlds most popular instrument, the guitar, is not taught in our public schools. In addition, it is one of the hardest on which to learn the basics of music. As a result, it is frequently difficult for the serious guitarist to get a firm foundation in theory.

Theory Workbook for Guitar Volume 1
Perfect Bound ISBN 1890944-52-1

This book provides real hands-on application of intervals and chords. A theory section written in concise and easy to understand language prepares the student for all exercises. Worksheets are given that quiz a student about intervals and chord construction using staff notation and guitar tablature. Answers are supplied in the back of the book enabling a student to work without a teacher.

Theory Workbook for Guitar Volume 2
Perfect Bound ISBN 1890944-53-X

This book provides real hands-on application for 22 different scale types. A theory section written in concise and easy to understand language prepares the student for all exercises. Worksheets are given that quiz a student about scale construction using staff notation and guitar tablature. Answers are supplied in the back of the book enabling a student to work without a teacher. Audio files are also available on the muse-eek.com website to facilitate practice and improvisation with all the scales presented.

Rhythm Book Series

These books are a breakthrough in music instruction, using the internet as a teaching tool! Audio files of all the exercises are easily downloaded from the internet.

Rhythm Primer
Perfect Bound ISBN 1890944-59-9

This 61 page book concentrates on all basic rhythms using four rhythmic levels. All examples use one pitch, allowing the student to focus completely on time and rhythm. All exercises can be downloaded from the internet to facilitate learning. See http://www.muse-eek.com for details

Rhythms Volume 1
Perfect Bound ISBN 1890944-55-6

This 120 page book concentrates on eighth note rhythms and is a thesaurus of rhythmic patterns. All examples use one pitch, allowing the student to focus completely on time and rhythm. All exercises can be downloaded from the internet to facilitate learning. See http://www.muse-eek.com for details.

Rhythms Volume 2
Perfect Bound ISBN 1890944-56-4

This volume concentrates on sixteenth note rhythms, and is a 108 page thesaurus of rhythmic patterns. All examples use one pitch, allowing the student to focus completely on time and rhythm. All exercises can be downloaded from the internet to facilitate learning. See http://www.muse-eek.com for details.

Rhythms Volume 3
Perfect Bound ISBN 1890944-57-2

This volume concentrates on thirty second note rhythms, and is a 102 page thesaurus of rhythmic patterns. All examples use one pitch, allowing the student to focus completely on time and rhythm. All exercises can be downloaded from the internet to facilitate learning. See http://www.muse-eek.com for details.

Odd Meters Volume 1
Perfect Bound ISBN 1890944-58-0

This book applies both eighth and sixteenth note rhythms to odd meter combinations. All examples use one pitch, allowing the student to focus completely on time and rhythm. Exercises can be downloaded from the internet to facilitate learning. This 100 page book is an essential sight reading tool. See http://www.muse-eek.com for details.

Contemporary Rhythms Volume 1
Perfect Bound ISBN 1890944-84-X

This volume concentrates on eight note rhythms and is a thesaurus of rhythmic patterns. Each exercise uses one pitch which allows the student to focus completely on time and rhythm. Exercises use modern innovations common to twentieth century notation, thereby familiarizing the student with the most sophisticated systems likely to be encountered in the course of a musical career. All exercises can be downloaded from the internet to facilitate learning. See http://www.muse-eek.com for details.

Contemporary Rhythms Volume 2
Perfect Bound ISBN 1890944-85-8

This volume concentrates on sixteenth note rhythms and is a thesaurus of rhythmic patterns. Each exercise uses one pitch which allows the student to focus completely on time and rhythm. Exercise use modern innovations common to twentieth century notation, thereby familiarizing the student with the most sophisticated systems likely to be encountered in the course of a musical career. All exercises can be downloaded from the internet to facilitate learning. See http://www.muse-eek.com for details.

Independence Volume 1
Perfect Bound ISBN 1890944-83-1

This 51 page book is designed for pianists, stick and touchstyle guitarists, percussionists and anyone who wishes to develop the rhythmic independence of their hands. This volume concentrates on quarter, eighth and sixteenth note rhythms and is a thesaurus of rhythmic patterns. The exercises in this book gradually incorporate more and more complex rhythmic patterns making it an excellent tool for both the beginning and the advanced student.

Other Guitar Study Aids

Right Hand Technique for Guitar Volume 1
Perfect Bound ISBN 1890944-54-8

Heres a breakthrough in music instruction, using the internet as a teaching tool! This book gives a concise method for developing right hand technique on the guitar, one of the most overlooked and under-addressed aspects of learning the instrument. The simplest, most basic movements are used to build fatigue-free technique. Exercises can be downloaded from the internet to facilitate learning. See http://www.muse-eek.com for details.

Single String Studies Volume One
Perfect Bound ISBN 1890944-62-9

This book is an excellent learning tool for both the beginner who has no experience reading music on the guitar, and the advanced student looking to improve their ledger line reading and general knowledge of each string of the guitar. Each exercise concentrates the students attention on one string at a time. This allows a familiarity to form between the written pitch and where it can be found on the guitar along with improving ones feel for jumping linearly across the fretboard. Exercises can be downloaded from the internet to facilitate learning. See http://www.muse-eek.com for details.

Single String Studies Volume Two
Perfect Bound ISBN 1890944-64-5

This book is a continuation of Volume One, but using non-diatonic notes. Volume Two helps the intermediate and advanced student improve their ledger line reading and general knowledge of each string of the guitar. Each exercise concentrates the students attention on one string at a time. This allows a familiarity to form between the written pitch and where it can be found on the guitar along with improving ones feel for jumping linearly across the fretboard. Exercises can be downloaded from the internet to facilitate learning. See http://www.muse-eek.com for details.

Single String Studies Volume One (Bass Clef)
Perfect Bound ISBN 1890944-63-7

This book is an excellent learning tool for both the beginner who has no experience reading music on the bass guitar, and the advanced student looking to improve their ledger line reading and general knowledge of each string of the bass. Each exercise concentrates a students attention of one string at a time. This allows a familiarity to form between the written pitch and where it can be found on the bass along with improving ones feel for jumping linearly across the fretboard. Exercises can be downloaded from the internet to facilitate learning. See http://www.muse-eek.com for details.

Single String Studies Volume Two (Bass Clef)
Perfect Bound ISBN 1890944-65-3

This book is a continuation of Volume One, but using non-diatonic notes. Volume Two helps the intermediate and advanced student improve their ledger line reading and general knowledge of each string of the bass. Each exercise concentrates the students attention on one string at a time. This allows a familiarity to form between the written pitch and where it can be found on the bass along with improving ones feel for jumping linearly across the fretboard. Exercises can be downloaded from the internet to facilitate learning. See http://www.muse-eek.com for details.

Guitar Clinic
Perfect Bound ISBN 1890944-86-6

Guitar Clinic contains techniques and exercises Mr. Arnold uses in the clinics and workshops he teaches around the U.S.. Much of the material in this book is culled from Mr. ArnoldÕs educational series, over thirty books in all. The student wishing to expand on his or her studies will find suggestions within the text as to which of Mr. Arnold's books will best serve their specific needs. Topics covered include: how to read music, sight reading, reading rhythms, music theory, chord and scale construction, modal sequencing, approach notes, reharmonization, bass and chord comping, and hexatonic scales.

The Essentials: Chord Charts, Scales, and Lead Patterns for the Guitar
Saddle Stitched (Stapled) ISBN 1-890944-94-7

This book is truly essential to the aspiring guitarist. It includes the most commonly played chords on the guitar in all keys, plus a bonus of the most commonly used scales and lead patterns. You can quickly learn all the chords, scales and lead patterns you need to know to play your favorite songs-and solo over them, too! The Essentials doesn't stop there, though. It also includes chord progressions to help you learn how to chord songs in folk, country, rock, blues and other popular styles. The books contain loads of easy to understand diagrams of chords, scales and lead patterns so you will be up and running in no time!

Sight Singing and Ear Training Series

The world is full of ear training and sight reading books, so why do we need more? This sight singing and ear training series uses a different method of teaching relative pitch sight singing and ear training. The success of this method has been remarkable. Along with a new method of ear training these books also use CDs and the internet as a teaching tool! Midifiles of many exercises are easily downloaded from the internet at www. muse-eek.com By combining interactive audio files with a new approach to ear training a student's progress is limited only by their willingness to practice!

A Fanatic's Guide to Ear Training and Sight Singing
Perfect Bound ISBN 1890944-75-0

This book and separately available CD present a method for developing good pitch recognition through sight singing. This method differs from the myriad of other sight singing books in that it develops the ability to identify and name all twelve pitches within a key center. Through this method a student gains the ability to identify sound based on it's relationship to a key and not the relationship of one note to another (i.e. interval training as commonly taught in many texts). All note groupings from one to six notes are presented giving the student a thesaurus of basic note combinations which develops sight singing and note recognition to a level unattainable before this Guide's existence.

Key Note Recognition
Perfect Bound ISBN 1890944-77-7

This book and separately available CD present a method for developing the ability to recognize the function of any note against a key. This method is a must for anyone who wishes to sound one note on an instrument or voice and instantly know what key a song is in. Through this method a student gains the ability to identify a sound based on its relationship to a key and not the relationship of one note to another (i.e. interval training as commonly taught in many texts). Key Center Recognition is a definite requirement before proceeding to two note ear training.

LINES Volume One: Sight Reading and Sight Singing Exercises
Perfect Bound ISBN 1890944-76-9

This book can be used for many applications. It is an excellent source for easy half note melodies that a beginner can use to learn how to read music or for sight singing slightly chromatic lines. An intermediate or advanced student will find exercises for multi-voice reading. These exercises can also be used for multi-voice ear training. The book has the added benefit in that all exercises can be heard by downloading the audio files for each example. See http://www.muse-eek.com for details.

LINES Volume Two: Sight Reading and Sight Singing Exercises
Perfect Bound ISBN 1594899-99-1

Recommended for those who have completed volume one, volume two introduces more complex harmonic material. This book can be used for many applications. It is an excellent source for easy quarter note melodies that a beginner can use to learn how to read music or for sight singing slightly chromatic lines. An intermediate or advanced student will find exercises for multi-voice reading. These exercises can also be used for multi-voice ear training. The book has the added benefit in that all exercises can be heard by downloading the audio files for each example. See http://www.muse-eek.com for details.

Ear Training ONE NOTE: Beginning Level
Perfect Bound ISBN 1890944-66-1

This Book and separately available audio CD present a new and exciting method for developing relative pitch ear training. It has been used with great success and is now finally available on CD. There are three levels available depending on the student's ability. This beginning level is recommended for students who have little or no music training.

Ear Training ONE NOTE: Intermediate Level
Perfect Bound ISBN 1890944-67-X

This book and separately available audio CD present a new and exciting method of developing relative pitch ear training. It has been used with great success and is now finally available on CD. This intermediate level is recommended for students who have had some music training but still find their skills need more development.

Ear Training ONE NOTE: Advanced Level
Perfect Bound ISBN 1890944-68-8

This book and separately available audio CD present a new and exciting method of developing relative pitch ear training. It has been used with great success and is now finally available on CD. There are three levels available depending on the student's ability. This advanced level is recommended for students who have worked with the intermediate level and now wish to perfect their skills.

Ear Training TWO NOTE: Beginning Level Volume One
Perfect Bound ISBN 1890944-69-6

This Book and separately available audio CD continues the method of developing relative pitch ear training as set forth in the "Ear Training, One Note" series. There are six volumes in the beginning level series. Through practice, the student eventually gains the ability to recognize the key and the names of any two notes played simultaneously. Volume One concentrates on 5ths. Prerequisite: a strong grasp of the One Note method.

Ear Training TWO NOTE: Beginning Level Volume Two
Perfect Bound ISBN 1890944-70-X

This Book and separately available audio CD continues the method of developing relative pitch ear training as set forth in the "Ear Training, One Note" series. There are six volumes in the beginning level series. Through practice, the student eventually gains the ability to recognize the key and the names of any two notes played simultaneously. Volume Two concentrates on 3rds. Prerequisite: a strong grasp of the One Note method.

Ear Training TWO NOTE: Beginning Level Volume Three
Perfect Bound ISBN 1890944-71-8

This Book and separately available audio CD continues the method of developing relative pitch ear training as set forth in the "Ear Training, One Note" series. There are six volumes in the beginning level series. Through practice, the student eventually gains the ability to recognize the key and the names of any two notes played simultaneously. Volume Three concentrates on 6ths. Prerequisite: a strong grasp of the One Note method.

Ear Training TWO NOTE: Beginning Level Volume Four
Perfect Bound ISBN 1890944-72-6

This Book and separately available audio CD continues the method of developing relative pitch ear training as set forth in the "Ear Training, One Note" series. There are six volumes in the beginning level series. Through practice, the student eventually gains the ability to recognize the key and the names of any two notes played simultaneously. Volume Four concentrates on 4ths. Prerequisite: a strong grasp of the One Note method.

Ear Training TWO NOTE: Beginning Level Volume Five
Perfect Bound ISBN 1890944-73-4

This Book and separately available audio CD continues the method of developing relative pitch ear training as set forth in the "Ear Training, One Note" series. There are six volumes in the beginning level series. Through practice, the student eventually gains the ability to recognize the key and the names of any two notes played simultaneously. Volume Five concentrates on 2nds. Prerequisite: a strong grasp of the One Note method.

Ear Training TWO NOTE: Beginning Level Volume Six
Perfect Bound ISBN 1890944-74-2

This Book and separately available audio CD continues the method of developing relative pitch ear training as set forth in the "Ear Training, One Note" series. There are six volumes in the beginning level series. Through practice, the student eventually gains the ability to recognize the key and the names of any two notes played simultaneously. Volume Six concentrates on 7ths. Prerequisite: a strong grasp of the One Note method.

Comping Styles Series

This series is built on the progressions found in Chord Workbook Volume One. Each book covers a specific style of music and presents exercises to help a guitarist, bassist or drummer master that style. Audio CDs are also available so a student can play along with each example and really get "into the groove."

Comping Styles for the Guitar Volume Two FUNK
Perfect Bound ISBN 1890944-60-2

This volume teaches a student how to play guitar or piano in a funk style. 36 Progressions are presented: 12 keys of a Major and Minor Blues plus 12 keys of Rhythm Changes A different groove is presented for each exercise giving the student a wide range of funk rhythms to master. A separately available audio CD is also included so a student can play along with each example and really get "into the groove." The audio CD contains "trio" versions of each exercise with Guitar, Bass and Drums.

Comping Styles for the Bass Volume Two FUNK
Perfect Bound ISBN 1890944-61-0

This volume teaches a student how to play bass in a funk style. 36 Progressions are presented: 12 keys of a Major and Minor Blues plus 12 keys of Rhythm Changes A different groove is presented for each exercise giving the student a wide range of funk rhythms to master. A separately available audio CD is also included so a student can play along with each example and really get "into the groove." The audio CD contains "trio" versions of each exercise with Guitar, Bass and Drums.

Jazz and Blues Bass Line
Perfect Bound ISBN 1890944-16-5

This book covers the basics of bass line construction. A theoretical guide to building bass lines is presented along with 36 chord progressions utilizing the twelve keys of a Major and Minor Blues, plus twelve keys of Rhythm Changes. A reharmonization section is also provided which demonstrates how to reharmonize a chord progression on the spot. A separately available audio CD allows a student can play along with each example.

Time Series

The Doing Time series presents a method for contacting, developing and relying on your internal time sense: This series is an excellent resource for any musician who is serious about developing strong internal sense of time. This is particularly useful in any kind of music where the rhythms and time signatures may be very complex or free, and there is no conductor.

THE BIG METRONOME
Spiral Bound ISBN 1-890944-37-8   Perfect Bound ISBN 1890944-82-3

The Big Metronome is designed to help you develop a better internal sense of time. This is accomplished by requiring you to "feel time" rather than having you rely on the steady click of a metronome. The idea is to slowly wean yourself away from an external device and rely on your internal/natural sense of time. The exercises presented work in conjunction with the three separately available CDs. CD 1 presents the first 13 settings from a traditional metronome 40-66; the second CD contains metronome markings 69-116, and the third CD contains metronome markings 120-208. The first CD gives you a 2 bar count off and a click every measure, the second CD gives you a 2 bar count off and a click every 2 measures, the 3rd CD gives you a 2 bar count off and a click every 4 measures. By presenting all common metronome markings a student can use these 3 CDs as a replacement for a traditional metronome.

Doing Time with the Blues Volume One
Perfect Bound ISBN 1890944-78-5

The book and separately available CD presents a method for gaining an internal sense of time thereby eliminating dependence on a metronome. The book presents the basic concept for developing good time and also includes exercises that can be practiced with the CD. The CD provides eight 8 minute tracks at different tempos in which the time is delineated every 2 bars, and with an extra hit every 12 bars to outline the blues form. The student may then use the exercises presented in the book to gain control of their execution or improvise to gain control of their ideas using this bare minimum of time delineation.

Doing Time with the Blues Volume Two
Perfect Bound ISBN 1890944-79-3

This is the 2nd volume of a four volume series which presents a method for developing a musicians internal sense of time, thereby eliminating dependence on a metronome. This 2nd volume presents different exercises which further the development of this time sense. This 2nd volume begins to test even a professional level players ability. The separately available CD provides eight 8 minute tracks at different tempos in which the time is delineated every 4 bars with an extra hit every 12 bars to outline the blues form. New exercises are also included that can be practiced with the CD. This series is an excellent resource for any musician who is serious about developing an internal sense of time.

Doing Time with 32 Bars Volume One
Perfect Bound ISBN 1890944-80-7

The book and separately available CD presents a method for gaining an internal sense of time thereby eliminating dependence on a metronome. The book presents the basic concept for developing good time and also includes exercises that can be practiced with the CD. The CD provides eight 8 minute tracks at different tempos in which the time is delineated every 2 bars, with an extra hit every 32 to outline the 32 bar form. The student may then use the exercises presented in the book to gain control of their execution or improvise to gain control of their ideas using this bare minimum of time delineation.

Doing Time with 32 Bars Volume Two
Perfect Bound ISBN 1890944-81-5

This is the 2nd volume of a four volume series which presents a method for developing a musicians internal sense of time, thereby eliminating dependence on a metronome.. This 2nd volume presents different exercises which further the development of this time sense. This 2nd volume begins to test even a professional level players ability. The separately available CD provides eight 8 minute tracks at different tempos in which the time is delineated every 4 bars with an extra hit every 32 bars to outline the 32 bar form. New exercises are also included that can be practiced with the CD. This series is an excellent resource for any musician who is serious about developing an internal sense of time.

Time Transformation
Perfect Bound ISBN 1594899-930-4

"Time Transformation" is designed to take the application of odd meters to another level of mastery. Etudes are presented in 12 keys using the time signatures of 3/4, 4/4, 5/4, 6/4 and 7/4. There are a total of 60 highly syncopated studies that are presented using various combinations of eighth note and sixteenth note rhythms. Book also includes downloadable "vamps" that can be used in various ways with each étude.

Other Workbooks

Music Theory Workbook for All Instruments, Volume 1: Interval and Chord Construction
Perfect Bound ISBN 1890944-46-7

This book provides real hands-on application of intervals and chords. A theory section written in concise and easy to understand language prepares the student for all exercises. Worksheets are given that quiz a student about intervals and chord construction using staff notation. Answers are supplied in the back of the book enabling a student to work without a teacher.

Jazz Piano Vocabulary by Roberta Piket, Volume 1: The Major Scale
Perfect Bound ISBN 1594899-51-7

This is the 1st volume in a series designed to help the student of jazz piano learn and apply jazz scales by mastering each scale and its uses in improvisation. Each book focuses on a different scale, illustrating the scale in all twelve keys with complete fingerings. Also provided are chords and left hand voicings to match, exercises and études to apply the material to improvising, ideas for further study and listening, and detailed suggestions on how to prace the material. Volume 1 also includes a detailed primer in note reading, basic theory, and rhythmic notation.

Jazz Piano Vocabulary by Roberta Piket, Volume 2: The Dorian Mode
Perfect Bound ISBN 1890944-98-X

The 2nd volume in the series, this book focuses on the Dorian scale and applies it to improvising on minor seventh chords. The Dorian scale is presented in all twelve keys with complete fingerings. The book also contains left hand voicings, exercises, many examples, an étude to help apply the material, ideas for further study, an extended discography, and detailed instruction and practice tips.

Jazz Piano Vocabulary by Roberta Piket, Volume 3: The Phrygian Mode
Perfect Bound ISBN 1594899-54-1

For students who have covered the basics in Volume 1,2 and 5, this book focuses in the Phrygian and Spanish Phrygian scales. It discusses "modern" jazz chords such as the "Phrygian" chord (susb9). The scale is presented in all 12 keys with fingerings. It also provides a detailed treatise on a modal approach to chord voicings, practice tips and a Phrygian étude.

Jazz Piano Vocabulary by Roberta Piket, Volume 4: The Lydian Mode
Perfect Bound ISBN 1594899-56-8

Volume 4 features the Lydian scale in all twelve keys; two octaves up and down with complete piano fingerings. Chords are presented with left hand voicings that work with the scale (along with fingerings) Also included are exercises to develop the concept of melodic phrasing in improvisation, examples of the use of the Lydian scale in the jazz repertoire, and detailed instructions on how to practice the material. Added feature: author can be contacted online if questions arise.

Jazz Piano Vocabulary by Roberta Piket, Volume 5: The Mixolydian Mode
Perfect Bound ISBN 1594899-58-4

This book focuses on the Mixolydian scale and applies it to improvising on dominant seventh and dominant seventh sus chords. The scale is presented in all twelve keys with fingerings. The book also contains an introduction to approach notes, an explanation and étude on twelve bar blues form, left hand voicings, exercises, melodic examples, instruction and practice tips.

Guitar Method Series

This series of books distills several of our previous publications into a method currently in use at New York University for the Summer Guitar Intensive Program. Content is geared towards any musician that is looking to expand their understanding of typical musical concepts but also covers many musically uncharted territories. Material concentrates on essential information the student must master in order to become a professional guitarist in the heavily competitive New York City music scene. This series of books starts with the most basic beginning guitar information and takes the reader to the most advanced musical concepts.

New York Guitar Method Primer Book 1
Perfect Bound ISBN 159489-912-6

This book provides students with an excellent foundation in theory, ear training, chord and scale comprehension on the guitar. It is a prerequisite for entering New York University's Summer Guitar Intensive Program and provides students studying independently with the tools they will need to successfully move on to Primer Book 2.

New York Guitar Method Primer Book 2
Perfect Bound ISBN 159489-916-9

This book provides students with an excellent foundation in theory, ear training, chord and scale comprehension on the guitar. It is a prerequisite for entering New York University's Summer Guitar Intensive Program and provides students studying independently with the tools they will need to successfully move on to New York Guitar Method Book 1. "New York Guitar Method Primer Ensemble Book Two" is the companion book for "New York Guitar Method Primer Book Two." This book contains music examples of the information covered in this book so that a student can apply the information through memorization and sight reading.

New York Guitar Method Primer Ensemble Book 2
Perfect Bound ISBN 159489-914-2

This book is a prerequisite for entering New York University's Summer Guitar Intensive Program and provides students studying independently with the tools they will need to successfully move on to Volume 1. Our Ensemble Method presents a breakthrough approach for teaching guitarist how to sightread. Each chapter has eighth note, sixteenth note, single string, lines, and chord exercises. The book also includes modal jazz vamps and solos and is an excellent resource for lab/ensemble studies as it contains 3 and 4-part reading examples.

New York Guitar Method Volume 1
Perfect Bound ISBN 159489-900-2

This book contains 22 scales and their theory which are covered in great detail. Multiple types of chord voicings along with an in-Depth coverage of articulations. The application of scales through modal sequences is also explained. The following musical concepts are covered: Finding the Right Scale for Any Chord, Finding the Natural Scale Sound, Thinking the Way You Hear, Two to Eleven Note Scale Possibilities along with a list of 2,048 Scale Possibilities which contain the root. Slash Chords, Regular Chords and Slash Chords, Slash Chord Possibilities, Reharmonization Theory, Adding Tensions.
"New York Guitar Method Ensemble Book One" is the companion book for "New York Guitar Method Volume One." This book contains music examples of the information covered in this book so that a student can apply the information through memorization and sight reading.

New York Guitar Method Ensemble Book 1
Perfect Bound ISBN 159489-906-1

Volume One focuses on reading jazz solos that demonstrate the many uses of scales as discussed in the accompanying New York Guitar Method Volume 1. The book also includes jazz and classical reading études and is an excellent resource for lab/ensemble studies as it contains 3 and 4-part reading examples.

New York Guitar Method Volume 2
Perfect Bound ISBN 159489-902-9

This is the second book in our series currently in use at New York University for the Summer Guitar Intensive Program. A continuation of Volume 1, Volume 2 focuses on approach notes and discusses how to apply approaches to jazz lines in order to create the signature sounding lines of bebop through the contemporary sounding lines of the modern masters. "New York Guitar Method Ensemble Book Two" is the companion book for "New York Guitar Method Volume Two." This book contains music examples of the information covered in this book so that a student can apply the information through memorization and sight reading.

New York Guitar Method Ensemble Book 2
Perfect Bound ISBN 159489-908-8
Volume Two focuses on reading jazz solos that demonstrate the many uses of approach notes as discussed in the accompanying New York Guitar Method Volume 2. The book also includes jazz and classical reading études and is an excellent resource for lab/ensemble studies as it contains 3 and 4-part reading examples.

Set Theory Method

This series of books explores the relationships of post tonal theory to contemporary improvisation. It is meant to bridge the gap between jazz theory and contemporary set theory.

Sonic Resource Guide
Perfect Bound ISBN 159489-934-7

"Set Theory for Improvisation" examines the use and organization of pitch class sets for improvisation and composition. Two through twelve note pitch class sets are explored and their application to the harmony and melody shown through multiple examples. The companion series "Set Theory for Improvisation Ensemble" is recommended as both a overall musical development tool and as a sight reading gold mine. For all instruments.

Set Theory for Improvisation Ensemble Method

The ensemble method gives examples of applying post tonal theory to contemporary improvisation in the form of études. Each étude explores the melodic possibilities using various combinations of note groupings, rhythms, metric level, melodic range and density. There are 12 études in each book, one in each key which can be played over a variety of chords. These études range from highly diatonic to non-diatonic examples depending on the organization of the material. For all instruments.

Set Theory for Improvisation Ensemble Method: Hexatonic 027 027
Perfect Bound ISBN 159489-921-5

Set Theory for Improvisation Ensemble Method: Hexatonic 027 016
Perfect Bound ISBN 159489-923-1

Set Theory for Improvisation Ensemble Method: Hexatonic 027 026
Perfect Bound ISBN 159489-925-8

The Bruce Arnold series of instructional E-books is for the student who wishes to target specific areas of study that are of particular interest. Many of these books are excerpted from other larger texts. The excerpted source is listed for each book. These books are available on-line at www.muse-eek.com as well as at many e-tailers throughout the internet. These books can also be purchased in the traditional book binding format. (See the ISBN number for proper format)

Chord Velocity: Volume One, Learning to switch between chords quickly
E-book ISBN 1-890944-88-2

The first hurdle a beginning guitarist encounters is difficulty in switching between chords quickly enough to make a chord progression sound like music. This book provides exercises that help a student gradually increase the speed with which they change chords. Special free audio files are also available on the muse-eek.com website to make practice more productive and fun. Within a few weeks, remarkable improvement can be achieved using this method. This book is excerpted from "1st Steps for a Beginning Guitarist Volume One."

Guitar Technique: Volume One, Learning the basics to fast, clean, accurate and fluid performance skills.
E-book ISBN 1-890944-91-2

This book is for both the beginning guitarist or the more experienced guitarist who wishes to improve their technique. All aspects of the physical act of playing the guitar are covered, from how to hold a guitar to the specific way each hand is involved in the playing process. Pictures and videos are provided to help clarify each technique. These pictures and videos are either contained in the book or can be downloaded at www. muse-eek.com This book is excerpted from "1st Steps for a Beginning Guitarist Volume One."

Accompaniment: Volume One, Learning to Play Bass and Chords Simultaneously
E-book ISBN 1-890944-87-4

The techniques found within this book are an excellent resource for creating and understanding how to play bass and chords simultaneously in a jazz or blues style. Special attention is paid to understanding how this technique is created, thereby enabling the student to recreate this style with other pieces of music. This book is excerpted from the book "Guitar Clinic."

Beginning Rhythm Studies: Volume One, Learning the basics of reading rhythm and playing in time.
E-book ISBN 1-890944-89-0

This book covers the basics for anyone wishing to understand or improve their rhythmic abilities. Simple language is used to show the student how to read and play rhythm. Exercises are presented which can accelerate the learning process. Audio examples in the form of midifiles are available on the muse-eek. com website to facilitate learning the correct rhythm in time. This book is excerpted from the book "Rhythm Primer."

www.ingramcontent.com/pod-product-compliance
Lightning Source LLC
Chambersburg PA
CBHW062055090426
42740CB00016B/3145